Help to W

by Jilly Hunt
Illustrated by Gustavo Mazali

Contents

OXFORD
UNIVERSITY PRESS

Meet Paul!

Paul

Paul likes: bikes, wheelchair sports

I am a sports coach.

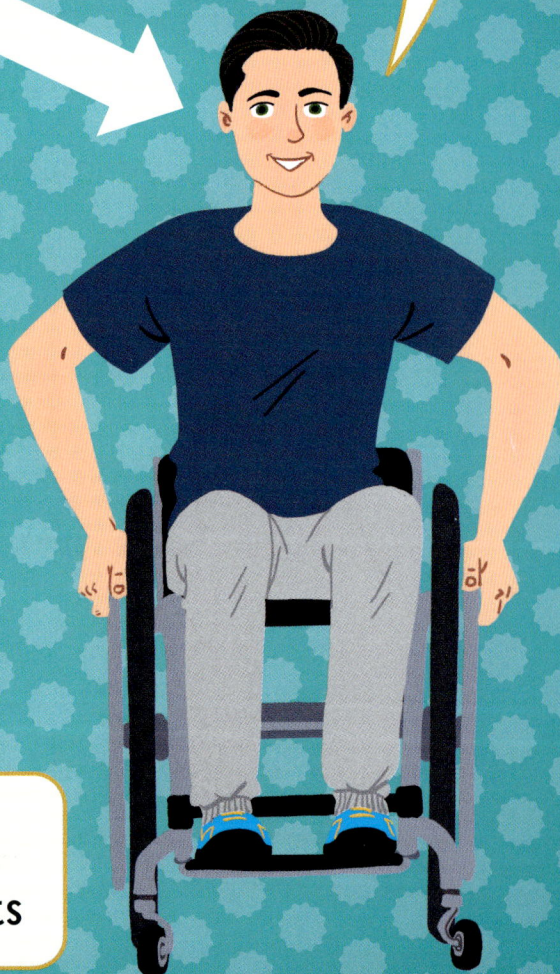

Paul came first at a few big bike events.
He was a champ!

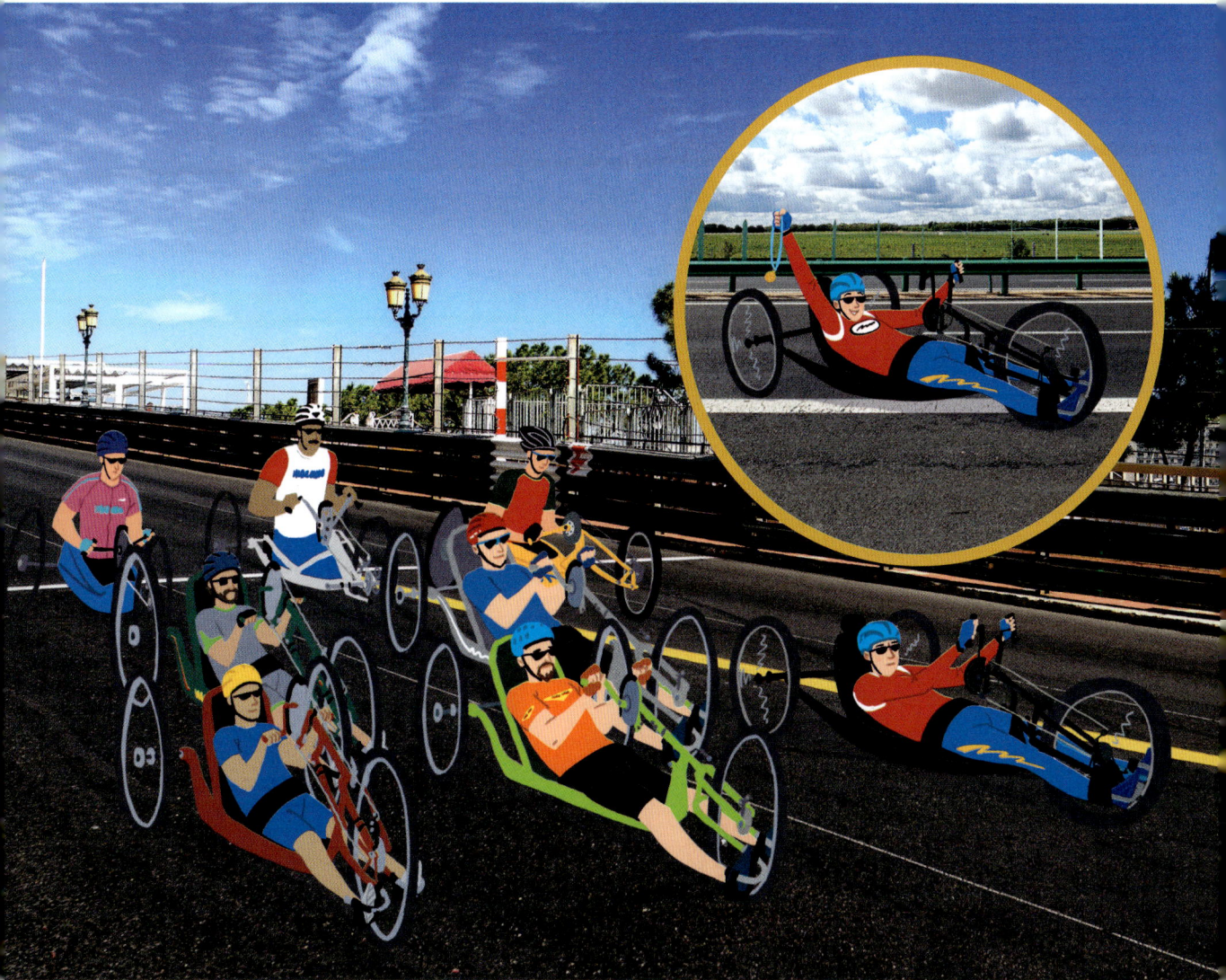

People asked Paul to help *them* be champs, too!

What is a sports coach?

A sports coach helps **athletes** to get better at their sport.

Philip

Paul had to **train** to be a sports coach.

Audrey

Now he trains athletes to do their best!

Joe

Training plans

A sports coach helps to make a **training plan** for each athlete.

I made this new plan for you.

The plan includes:

what to eat ...

how to keep fit ...

when to train ...

when to take time off.

You can do it!

Paul trains athletes to keep going, even when it's hard.

He gets them to think of their **goals**. He tells them not to quit.

Paul tells athletes that they must have fun, too!

Time to take part

Paul goes to events to see his athletes **compete**.
He tells them to enjoy it!

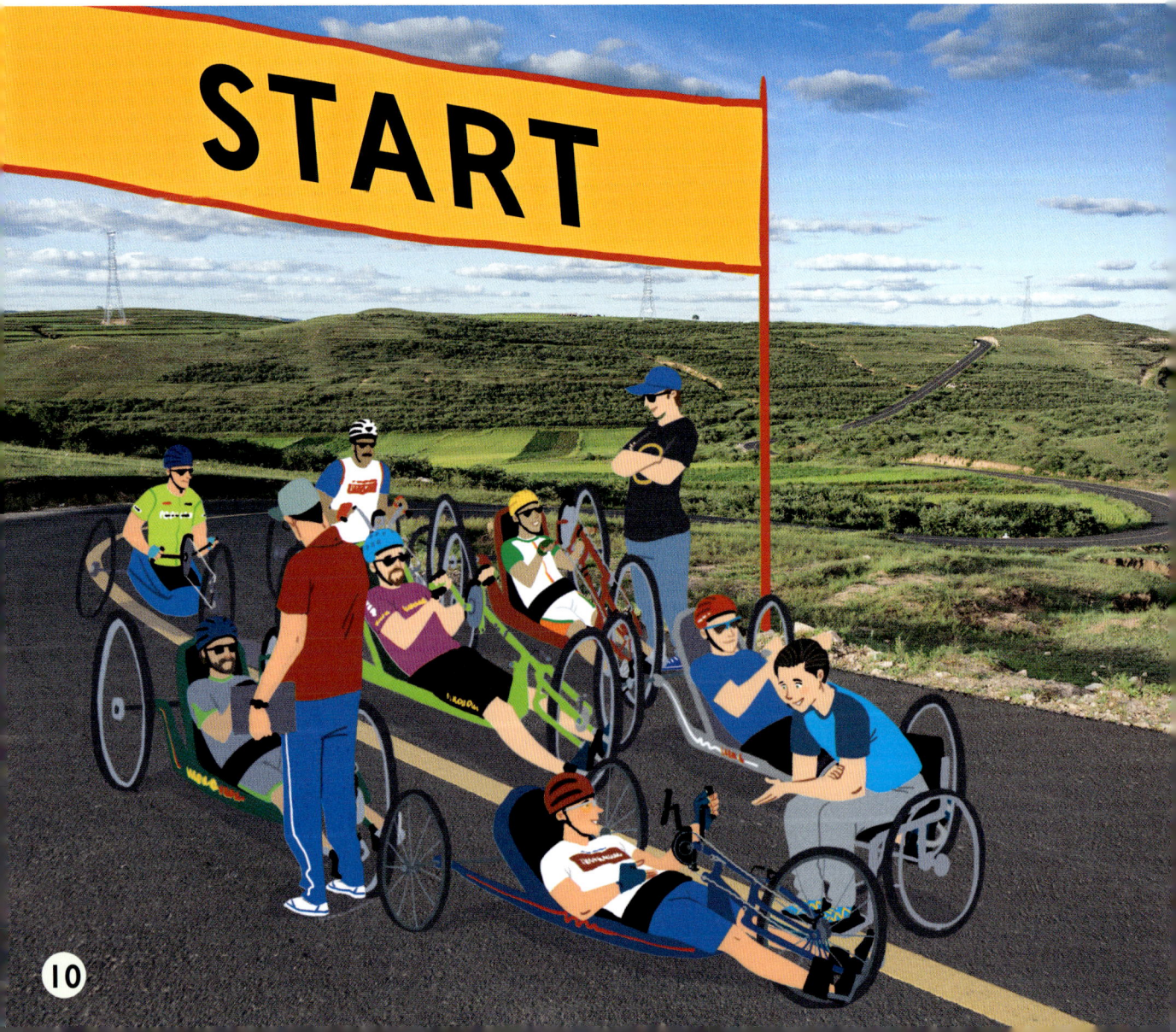

Paul whoops out loud when they win!
He likes it when they take home a prize.

Dealing with defeat

It can be hard for athletes when they do not win. They feel sad.

Paul explains that they need to keep training.

Even the best athletes make mistakes.

Tips

Paul hopes he can help all athletes to do their best.

Paul's key training tips

- Never quit.
- Be brave.
- Train hard.
- Do not be late.
- Take time to rest.
- Use mistakes to help you get better.
- Take pride in what you do.

Look it up!

athletes	people good at sport
compete	to take part in an event and aim to win it
goals	things that you hope to do
train	to do a thing lots of times to get better at it
training plan	a list of things to do to help you get better at a sport

Index

The *Look it up!* section is also called a Glossary. You can use it to look up the meanings of words that are in **bold** in this book. The Index will help you find key information.